i

If your young reader enjoys reading *You are too Young*, then be sure to look for *Rhue's House* as your child develops into a lifelong reader.

In *Rhue's House*, Rhue slides into a heart-warming romance with Thomas when her younger brother Hank, who is considered "odd," makes a connection with recent widower George. Rhue's father permits the relationship because of the benefits to young Hank.

Rhue's and Thomas' romance is not the only one that results from this new connection. Through her new relationship with George, Rhue gains access to Maggie's library. Emerging herself into the pages of Maggie's journals, Rhue develops a deep love for the couple as she reads about their life together.

However, not everything in Rhue's life is as perfect as it appears. When Maggie's journals reveal a deep family secret, Rhue discovers that her family has been deceiving her for her entire life.

You are too Young!

You are too Young!

Shannon W. Helzer

Twin Oars Publishing

Contents

This book is dedicated to the following very special individuals

For Elijah and Immanuel. You two are the greatest children in the world. You are also fine people. It is an honor to be your father, your Papa.

Ted. Thank you for your friendship and your support. You are a great teacher. Thank you for teaching my sons and me some of the finer points of wood working and craftsmanship.

Vanessa. Thank you for your support. Thank you also for encouraging me to build the barn with Immanuel and to write this story.

Zachary and Alyssa. Thank you for letting me be Augustus Mudiwa's Grandfather!

Chapter 1

You are too young!

Shannon W. Helzer

Hello everyone. My name is Immanuel. My friends call me Manny. I am six years old. There are many things that you may know about me, but there is one thing that I know about myself. I am "too young!"

You know how it is. For instance, when I say that I want to cook like my brother, my Papa always says…

"You are too young!"

3

Shannon W. Helzer

When I want to drive a car like my brother, my Papa always says...

"You are too young!"

When I want to go hunting like my brother, my Papa always says...

"You are too young!"

"You are too young!"

"You are too young!"

"You are too young!"

It was the same thing last summer when my Papa built some furniture for our new house. He made a trestle table and benches, a desk, a coffee table, and some picture frames. As usual, my brother Elijah got to help. When I asked if I could help to build the furniture, guess what he said.

"You are too young!"

"You are too young!"

<u>"You are too young!"</u>

It is just not fair. Papa showed Elijah how to use a **rasp** to file away some of the wood from a trestle for the table.

A **rasp** is a coarse metal tool with a roughened surface used to scrape, file, or rub down wood.

Mr. Shaffer showed Elijah and Papa how to use a **mallet** and a **chisel** to make a hole through the leg for the trestle. Elijah did a great job and did not even make a mistake. Papa, on the other hand, made some mistakes!

Look at me. I am just standing there watching! "Why?" you may ask. Because Papa always says…

"You are too young!"

A carpenter uses a wood *mallet* when hammering chisels. A metal hammer could damage the end of a chisel.

A *chisel* is used to carve or cut away wood. A carpenter strikes the chisel with the mallet.

Elijah also got to use a **sander** to sand the legs of the trestle table.

Guess what was I doing while he used the sander.

That's right. I was just standing there! "Why?" you may ask. Because, my Papa always says…

"You are too young!"

A **sander** uses sandpaper, which is very rough to the touch, to smooth wood. There are several different types of sanders.

The one above is a palm sander, and the one below is a belt sander.

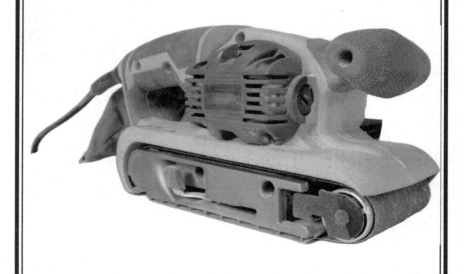

After using a sander, Elijah used a scroll saw to cut some smaller pieces of wood.

And, as usual, I just had to watch. "Why?" you may ask. Because Papa always says that...

"You are too young!"

"You are too young!"

"You are too young!"

Elijah and Papa worked for several weeks together. As always, I just had to watch because Papa always said, "You are too young!"

Finally, the day came when they were done. Whoopie doo dah day! Big whoop! I did not get to help because you know what Papa always says.

"You are too young!"

There was a surprise though. Papa and Elijah made something special just for me. They made me a trestle table with benches that are just my size.

Chapter 2

I am not too young?

For a while there I forgot that Papa always says, "You are too young." Then one day while we were visiting Mr. Shafer's house, I saw him putting in a new stairway. Naturally, I asked him if I could help. Do you know what his answer was?

"Sorry, Manny, but....

"You are too young!"

How I hate being too young! I want to build something too! I can do it! I am not a baby! I am not too young!

I went to my Papa and said, "Papa, I want to build something."

"What would you like to build, Manny?" he asked.

I said that I did not know what I wanted to build, but that I knew that I could build something.

"Well," Papa said, "how about you and I work together to build a barn?"

Shannon W. Helzer

A barn, I thought. "A Barn?"

"Yes, Manny, we could build a barn. We could build a real Pennsylvania Dutch barn with Hex signs and everything," he said.

Were we really going to build a barn? Yes! We were really going to do it! Papa, Elijah, and I were going to build a barn!

And best of all, I was not too young!!

To start with we visited the "lumber yard" and "bought" our materials. We needed 2x6's, 8x8 poles, boards, and batting.

Ok, I know what you're thinking. "That's not enough material to build a barn."

Well, you are wrong. We are not building a full-sized barn; we are building a scaled down version. Papa cut the materials in Mr. Shaffer's wood shop. He cut them to be just the right size.

The first thing we did was to build the frame of the barn. I asked Papa to name the parts of the barn as we built it.

"Well, Manny," he started, "the vertical pieces are 8x8's known as either *poles* or *posts*, and the horizontal boards are 2x6's known as either *beams* or *girts*."

The barn's **posts** support the weight of the building.

The *girts* transfer the weight of the building to the posts.

Together, the posts and the girts make the barn's *frame*.

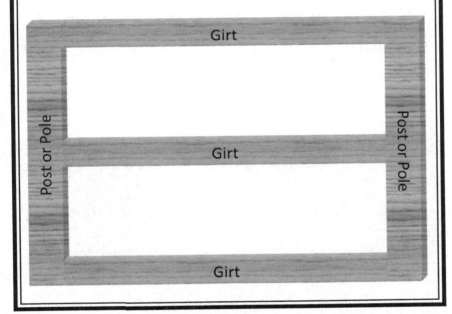

After we built the frame, we put on the boards that make up the **siding** of the barn. However, once we finished the **siding**, I noticed that there were some cracks in the barn between the siding boards.

"Papa," I asked, "what are we going to do about the cracks? Won't they let the rain and wind into the barn?"

"They would if we left them there," he answered.

"So, what are we going to do about them?" I asked.

"We are going to cover them with special boards known as **batting**," he explained. "The **batting** covers the cracks and makes the barn look pretty."

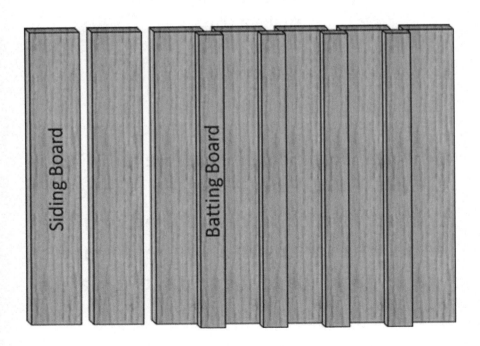

After we put on the barn's siding, we built the roof. We started by building the **trusses**.

"What are **trusses**, Papa?" I asked.

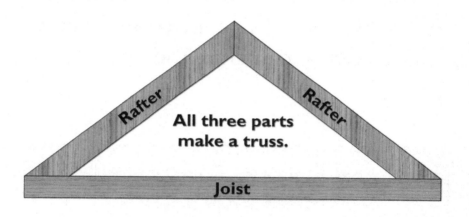

Rafter

Rafter

All three parts make a truss.

Joist

"They are the parts of the barn that hold up the roof," he answered. "You build trusses by connecting two identical **rafters** to a **joist**. When you are done, the triangular shaped trusses are evenly spaced across the barn's top girt."

Shannon W. Helzer

After we assembled and installed the **trusses** on top of the barn's **frame**, we needed to build the roof. "Are we going to put shingles on the roof?" I asked excitedly.

"No, Manny," he continued, "we are going to build the roof the way the Pennsylvania Dutch built their roofs. We are going to use large boards known as **ribbons**.

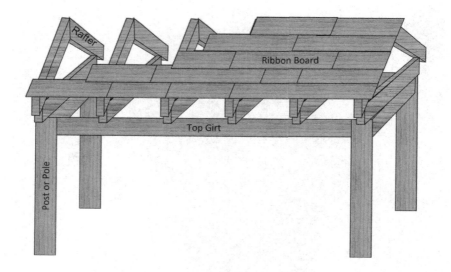

If you look closely, then you can see the ribboned roof on the next page.

After building the barn, we needed to paint the barn. That's my mom Vanessa. She is a professional interior designer. She helped us paint the barn. "Why are you putting tape on the barn?" I asked her.

"You put tape on the parts of the barn that you do not want to get paint on because later you will paint it a different color," she said while aligning the blue masking tape on the barn's roof.

When she finished applying the tape, it was time to paint the barn. "Are you going to paint the barn, Papa?" I asked.

"No, Manny, I am not going to paint. I am a bad painter," he answered.

"Is Vanessa going to paint the barn?" I continued.

"No, Manny, Vanessa is not going to paint the barn," he replied patiently.

"Who's going to paint the barn?" I asked.

"Why, you are Manny," he concluded.

"I am?" I asked. "But aren't I too young?"

"No, Manny, you are not too young," he said with a smile. "Here is the paint brush."

Paint brushes come in a wide variety of sizes. They are dipped into paint and brushed across the surface you wish to paint.

It took several hours to paint the barn. We had to be very careful with the details around the doors and the corners.

When we finished painting, the barn looked very real. "Wow, Papa, it looks really great!" I said. "Are we finished now?"

"Nope. We have one thing left to do," said Papa.

"What is that?" I asked.

"We need to put on the Pennsylvania Dutch Hex Signs," he answered.

Chapter 3

What are Hex Signs?

"Hex Signs?" I wondered out loud. "What are Hex Signs?"

"They are the colorful decorations we always see on the barns in the area where we live," he explained. "Hex Signs were used by the ancestors of the Pennsylvania German settlers who settled in Lehigh, Berks, and Lancaster counties. Now these signs are used as decorations on many barns across Pennsylvania."

We went online and looked up Pennsylvania Dutch Hex Signs. There were hundreds and hundreds of pretty signs.

"Wow," I said. "What signs will we pick for our barn?"

"Well," said Papa, "you are old enough to pick. Why don't you make the first selection?"

"Wow! I am old enough," I said. So, I looked. And I looked. And I looked. And I looked. And I looked again.

As I looked at my choices, Papa said, "Do you know that each sign and symbol has a meaning?"

Just then I saw the first one I liked. "Papa, I want the one with the uni-corns on it. What does it mean?"

"Well, according to the description," he answered, "princely unicorns pay tribute to the Dutch symbol of faith. The Unicorn provides piety, virtue, peace, and contentment."

I looked at him curiously for a moment. "Is that good?" I asked.

"Yes, Manny," he laughed, "that is very good! Can I pick one too?"

"Sure," I said, "which one do you like?"

"Since we have Irish ancestors," he began, "I like the Luck of the Irish hex sign. Did you know that many Irish became a part of the Pennsylvania Dutch through marriage? Pennsylvania has a very diverse history."

We looked for a while longer on many, many different web sites. We finally picked a third sign just because it was neat!

We printed out the signs we liked, glued them onto small round wooden circles, and mounted them on the barn.

We made a real 1:12 scale model of a barn. I was not too young! Papa and I worked for over four months, but we did it!

Check out how nice the barn looks! How cool is that?

This 1:12 scale model barn is exactly like the real one Papa built for Miss. Rhue on her farm. Papa also wrote a book about Rhue's life from the time she was a girl until she was in her 90's. The book is called **Rhue's House**.

Here are some pictures of Miss Rhue's house and farm just before she moved in. Do you see the red barn?

Chapter 4

The Barn

Now, let's take a trip to the inside of the barn. Here is what the barn looks like from the main entry doors.

We can even park my John Deere tractor inside of the barn.

If you look closely, then you can see the **poles** and **girts** in the walls and the **floor joist** for the hay mow above the tractor.

You can see the hay mow on the next page. The hay mow is the place where the farmer stores the hay for the year until it was needed by the animals on the farm. Animals like horses, cows, goats, and sheep eat the hay.

Check out the floorboards in the picture below! They are very pretty. They are nailed to the barn's floor joist.

If we look on the next page, then we can see the **trusses**. They are shaped like triangles.

The horizontal base of the triangle is the **ceiling joist**. The slanted beams are known as **rafters**.

Well, as you can see, I may be too young, but I am not too young to build a barn!

Hey, I have an idea. "Papa, follow me quick!"

"Where are we going?" Papa asked.

"Out to the truck," I answered. "Quick let me in!"

Papa opened the door to the truck, and I sat behind the steering wheel. I closed the door and looked out at Papa with a smile on my face. "Papa, can I drive the truck?"

"Manny," he started to say.

"I know, I know, Papa, ...

"I am too young!"

You win some, and you lose some!

Chapter 5

Your assignment

Papa and I built the barn model you just read about using what is known as Timber Frame Construction. This method uses posts and beams just like we did. Builders have used this technique to build homes and barns for hundreds of years.

You learned about many parts of timber framed buildings in this book!

And now you get to show how smart you are!

Did you notice the pictures in ovals, like the one below, at the bottom of some of the book's pages? These are pictures of Miss Rhue's house during the framing process.

Your assignment is to go back and to see if you can identify some of the parts in these pictures you have learned about. The parts we learned about include:

Rafters

Joist

Posts or Poles

Girts or Beams

Ribbon Boards

Batton Boards

Siding Boards

Trusses

Have fun doing your assignment! You can do it. Unless of course....

You are too Young!

Chapter 6

Tools, Tools, Tools!

Papa and I thought that this would be a good time to introduce other boys and girls to some tools that they might one day use for small carpentry projects.

The first tools are very important even though Papa forgot to have us wear them while we were working!

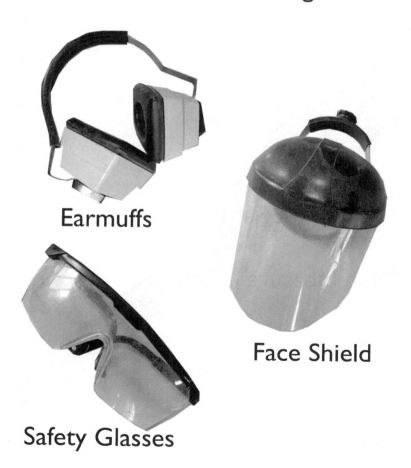

Earmuffs

Face Shield

Safety Glasses

Face shields and safety glasses keep wood chips from getting in your eyes when you use saws and chisels.

Earmuffs help keep your ears safe from loud noises made by the saws.

Tape measures help you measure the length of things when you build.

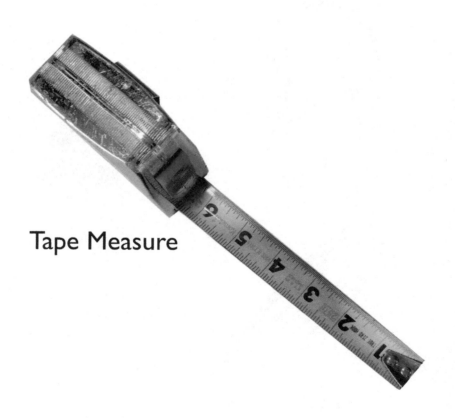

Tape Measure

Clamps and vices hold things in place when you work on them. Vices are bolted to heavy workbenches. Elijah used a vice on page 7 when he used a rasp. Look back to see how a vice is used.

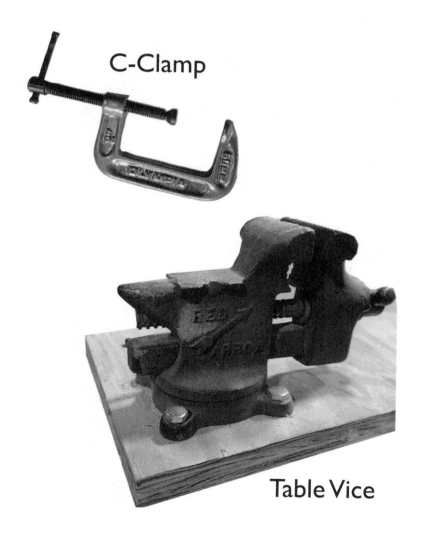

C-Clamp

Table Vice

Squares and bevel gauges are useful when you need to either draw or to measure angles.

Can you find the Speed Square in the picture on page 21?

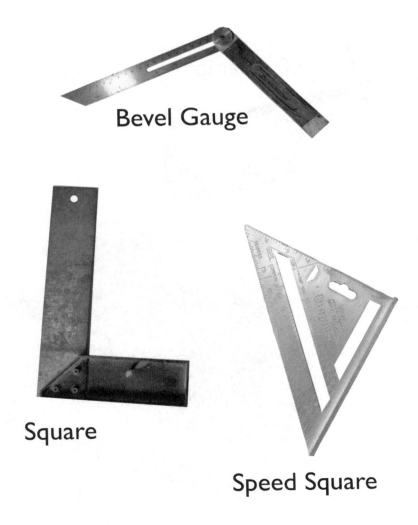

Bevel Gauge

Square

Speed Square

Sledge Hammer

Ball Peen
Hammer

Claw Hammer

Rubber
Mallet

My favorite tool is the hammer. There
are many different kinds of hammers.
A carpenter uses a hammer to direct
a lot of force at an object like a nail.
A hand hammer has a metal head
connected perpendicularly to a handle.

Fourteen Years Later...

There are few gifts in life more precious than children, yet we only have them for a very short period of time. Before we realize it, they are grown and on their own.

Fourteen years have already passed since I started this book. I am very thankful to have this snapshot of my sons' lives to remember the joys of being blessed with young children. Manny is on the left, and Elijah is on the right,

If you are in the midst of parenting young ones, then hang in there. Take every opportunity to enjoy your little ones. If that phase of life has slipped by for you or if you do not have children of your own, then reach out to a young parent or family that does. Your help will bless them and you much more than you ever thought possible.

The End!

Made in the USA
Columbia, SC
12 January 2023

10150178R00046